MEDIAWISE

ADVERTISING

Technology • People • Process

JULIAN PETLEY

Smart Apple Media

Media Wise series
Advertising   Film   Internet   Newspapers & Magazines

Produced for Hodder Wayland by Discovery Books Limited
Unit 3, 37 Watling Street, Leintwardine, Shropshire SY7 0LW, England

Editor: Patience Coster, Series editor: Victoria Brooker, Series design: Mind's Eye Design,
Commissioned photographs: Chris Fairclough

With thanks to all at Fox Murphy Marketing Communications, Norwich

Published in the United States by Smart Apple Media
1980 Lookout Drive, North Mankato, Minnesota 56003

Library of Congress Cataloging-in-Publication Data

Petley, Julian.
Advertising / by Julian Petley.
p. cm. — (Media wise)
Summary: Describes an advertising campaign from planning to completion, and profiles
various jobs in advertising, such as account executive, director, media planner, and
production assistant.
Includes bibliographical references and index.
ISBN 1-58340-255-1
1. Advertising—Juvenile literature. [1. Advertising—Vocational guidance. 2. Vocational
guidance.] I. Title. II. Series.

HF5829 .P48 2003
659.1—dc21   2002191171

9 8 7 6 5 4 3 2 1

Picture acknowledgments: The Advertising Archives 5, 7, 9, 12, 13, 14, 15, 16, 17, 18, 19, 42
(Rocher is a registered trademark of Ferrero); Benetton 24; Corbis 4 (Mark Stephenson), 8, 10,
21 (Nik Wheeler), 41, 45, 47 (Pablo Corral), 51 (Eric K.K. Yu), 57; Discovery Picture Library
11, 53, 58; Fox Murphy 20, 40, 46; Impact 48; Marysia Lachowicz 55.

Cover: Corbis (Mark Stephenson)

CONTENTS

What Is Advertising? **4**

Planning an Advertising Campaign **18**

How an Advertising Agency Works **25**

The Creative Process **30**

Buying Time and Space **38**

Production **49**

Getting a Job in the Industry **56**

Glossary **60**

Useful Addresses **61**

Books to Read **63**

Index **64**

WHAT IS ADVERTISING?

Advertising is the means by which goods or services are promoted to the public. The advertiser's goal is to increase sales of these goods or services by drawing people's attention to them and showing them in a favorable light. Early forms of advertising included the red-and-white striped pole that indicated a barber's shop, the three balls outside a pawnbroker's shop, and a sign such as "The King's Head" marking an inn. However, advertising as we know it today is a much more complicated and elaborate business, employing thousands of people with a wide range of skills in marketing, public relations, writing, photography, graphic design, filmmaking, and so on.

Many city streets, such as this one in Japan, glow with huge, neon-lit advertisements.

For advertising to exist, a number of factors have to be in place.

- The goods and services to be advertised
- Competition between different providers of the same kinds of goods and services, for which there needs to be a significant potential market
- The means of advertising cheaply to large numbers of people
- A population with sufficient education to be able to understand advertising messages

A growth industry

At the beginning of the 19th century, the main printed media—newspapers and magazines—were less important to advertisers than posters, handbills, tradespeople's "cards" listing their wares, "advertising engines" (horse-drawn wooden towers covered in posters), and the "sandwich men" who walked the streets with poster boards strapped to their bodies. However, by the middle of the century, newspapers and magazines were fast becoming the main sources for advertisers, as would commercial television and radio in the 20th century.

The sandwich man used to be a common sight in towns and cities.

Today we live in an image-saturated society, and advertisements account for a significant proportion of this media barrage. Researchers in the United States have estimated that by the age of 18, the average American will have seen some 350,000 commercials.

The first agencies

In Britain, William Tayler founded the first advertising agency in 1786. Better known, however, is the agency founded by James White around 1800, which specialized in official recruitment advertising. The first independent advertising agency in North America was established by Volney Palmer in Philadelphia in 1842.

However, advertisements take many forms other than television and radio commercials. In newspapers and magazines, large, bold "display" advertisements are used to promote the products and services of well-known commercial names. There are also the less conspicuous but much more numerous "classifieds" or "small ads" for cars, houses, and the like. Junk mail trying to sell us anything from windshields to credit cards pours into our mailboxes every day. In the streets, ads hail us from fences and the walls of buildings, or from the sides of buses and taxis. On our computer screens, eye-catching advertisements wink colorfully at us on an increasing number of Internet Web sites. In shopping centers, signs and flyers direct us to particular stores, and so on. It has been suggested that the average consumer is exposed to some 3,000 commercial messages of one kind or another each day.

The birth of the advertising agency

Originally, people wanting to advertise their goods and services designed their own advertisements and gave them to the relevant media for publication. Or they paid those already working in these media to design advertisements for them. However, it wasn't long before the design, creation, and placing of advertisements for those wishing to promote their goods or services came to be seen as a valuable financial opportunity in itself. In this way, the advertising agency was born.

An agency is a team of experts in all aspects of the advertising business that a client with a product or service to sell has traditionally employed to create advertisements and then to place them in a wide range of different media.

Although most major companies today employ advertising agencies, it is, of course, possible for individuals to advertise without going to the trouble and expense of involving an agency. For example, if you're selling your car through the local paper or the Internet, you don't need an agency to place the advertisement for you!

The first advertising agents simply sold space to advertisers in newspapers and magazines. Agents made a living from the fees they received from these publications in return, since these media paid the agents a percentage of the sale in commission. As the number and quality of publications increased, these agents began to compete with each other by offering to write and design their clients' advertisements, as well as placing them in the appropriate media. Having started off working for the media by selling advertising space, they ended up effectively working for the client by both buying and filling the advertising space they required.

Young people with money to spend on clothes and makeup are an important market for advertisers to reach.

HOLIDAY IS HERE

the chunky turtleneck

GAP

Soap operas

In the United States during the 1920s, numerous manufacturers began to sponsor radio programs—in other words, they financed their production. The same thing happened with television programs during the 1940s. The manufacturers' advertising agencies would actually produce the programs themselves. This system was the origin of the soap opera, so-called because these ongoing dramas were sponsored by laundry detergent manufacturers.

Companies are eager to advertise their latest innovations—and none more so than those involved in new forms of communication, such as the Internet.

Thus the "creative" agency developed, with advertisers increasingly buying space through the agencies that offered them the best ideas and services. The growth of newspapers and magazines, and later of cinema, radio, and television, contributed to the rapid development of the advertising industry by providing it with a vast number of new places in which to advertise, and huge potential audiences.

From the 1940s onward, the media scene became ever larger and more complex, and people who wanted to advertise their wares needed an increasing amount of expert help and advice. Large sections of the population were becoming more affluent, and a huge range of consumer goods and services was accordingly aimed at getting people to spend their money. From the sellers' point of view, this meant that there was a greater need than ever for effective advertising.

All these factors further encouraged the development of the "full service" agency, which—as the name implies—offered its clients an entire range of services, such as market and media research, advertisement design and production, planning campaigns, and buying advertising spaces in the different media. Some agencies also offered help and advice on marketing, promotional, and public relations activities.

A more intelligent way to get technology information. Online.

While the agencies grew in size and complexity, the advertising industry's clients became ever more global in reach. This was mainly because they had simply run out of new customers in their home markets and were increasingly eager to seek new ones abroad. As more of the clients became multinational—that is, they operated in a number of different countries—so the agencies began to follow suit. This led to many agencies becoming involved in joint global ventures with other agencies, and, in a number of cases, merging. A significant number of British agencies were bought up by American ones. Today a relatively small number of large firms, such as McCann-Erickson, J. Walter Thompson, Ogilvy & Mather, and Saatchi & Saatchi, dominate the international market.

New consumer appliances such as washing machines were heavily advertised in the 1950s.

The new media

The last two decades of the 20th century witnessed the development of entirely new forms of communication, as well as rapid and fundamental changes in the existing media. In European countries, an explosion in the number of new commercial channels was greatly aided by the development of cable and satellite broadcasting and of digital technology. Meanwhile, the fact that powerful computers were now cheap enough to enable many people to purchase them for home use gave a huge boost to new forms of communication such as sending e-mails and surfing the Internet. Advertisers were quick to spot the commercial possibilities of these and many other forms of new technology.

There is virtually no public, urban space that is not suited to carrying advertising.

There are now more media than ever in which to advertise, and competition between the media for advertising has never been more intense. In television terms, the days of the "mass" audience for a particular program such as *Friends* or *Survivor* may be drawing to a close. Advertisers may therefore become more wary of paying vast amounts of money to have their advertisements shown in what are currently regarded as the most popular viewing slots. As people watch a greater number of channels or turn to different forms of electronic media, advertisers in the future may well have to use many more media—and spend much more money—to reach audiences of this size. Meanwhile, others interested only in certain segments of the audience may decide to concentrate simply on various special-interest channels, such as those dedicated to movies, sports, or cartoons.

Above-the-line

In the advertising business, different forms of advertising have traditionally been divided into two separate categories: above-the-line and below-the-line. Originally, above-the-line advertising referred to advertisements placed by advertising agencies on behalf of their clients (in other words, those with goods and services to sell) in the press and cinema and on television and radio, as well as on outdoor sites of one kind or another. All of these media paid sums of money, known as "commission," to the agencies themselves, since the agencies were acting as useful intermediaries between those with something to sell and the media, saving the latter a great deal of time and trouble (and, of course, money).

Below-the-line

Meanwhile, below-the-line advertising included virtually everything else, especially forms of direct marketing such as letters and leaflets sent to potential consumers (often known as "junk mail"), brochures and posters displayed in shops, exhibitions, and so on. Those with goods and services to sell either produced such advertising themselves or paid agencies to do it for them. The important difference between above- and below-the-line advertising is that the former appear in the mainstream "mass" media that pay commission to advertising agencies, while the latter is a form of non-commissioned advertising targeted directly at a specific audience.

Branding

A lot of advertising today is part of a wider process known as marketing. In particular, large manufacturers make great use of advertising to create positive, distinctive, and readily identifiable "brand images" for their products.

Advertisements, such as this one in Chicago, are usually positioned to ensure that the maximum number of passers-by see them.

A brand image such as the instantly recognizable Volkswagen logo or the Nike "swoosh" differentiates a product from similar goods made by rival companies (such as Coca-Cola and Pepsi), and works to persuade customers to stay loyal to a particular brand.

Esso's longstanding use of the tiger in their advertising campaigns has resulted in it becoming closely associated with their particular brand of gas.

Advertisers may be private individuals or small businesses advertising in one medium at a very local level. Alternatively, they may be major producers, retailers (such as Sears or Wal-Mart), or service providers (such as Cellular One or American Airlines) advertising in all the media at the national or even global level. Recent years have seen a massive growth in the advertising of services of one kind or another, not least those financial ones offered by banks, insurance companies, and stockbrokers. At the same time, major retailers such as department stores and supermarket, electrical, and hardware chains are now advertising their ever-growing range of "own label" brands. In this way, they are, in a sense, selling themselves to a far greater extent than in the past, when they were more content simply to distribute and sell goods produced—and advertised—by others.

Market share

Today there are more products and services to advertise than ever before. In this saturated marketplace, manufacturers will put all their energies into a desperate bid simply to maintain their all-important "share" of the markets in which they operate. Given the vast sums of money involved here, even a small percentage loss of share can result in a massive decline in income to these companies.

The way in which companies have fought to maintain their market share has been to increase dramatically the number of brands they offer, and to try to cater to every imaginable "niche" of particular markets. Advertising plays a key role here, not simply in differentiating each of these brands from the others, but also in targeting the "right" kind of consumer for each brand.

This advertisement is carefully targeted at a very particular part of the youth market: young women who are into sports.

For this reason, advertisers are obsessed with identifying the components of people's varying "lifestyles" and then trying to manufacture the appropriate "brand images" for the products they are trying to sell. Perhaps this is why so many contemporary advertisements seem, on the surface at least, to give us so few hard facts about the products themselves! However, an advertisement that we admire as clever, artistic, or amusing may attract us to the brand by more subtle means. Whatever the case, it has been argued that the increased number of brands and the greater apparent choice between them has actually had the effect of weakening customer loyalty to a particular brand, and that advertising, however memorable in itself, has done little to halt this process.

This advertisement creates a glamorous brand image for fashion retailers Dolce & Gabbana. It appeals to style-conscious women by suggesting that buying the brand will help make them beautiful, chic, and smart.

Through-the-line

One outcome of these changes in both advertising and the media has been that those wishing to advertise their products and services have switched a good deal of their advertising budget into public relations, sponsorship, direct marketing, and sales promotions. With more media in which to advertise, the cost of advertising has risen alarmingly. Also, traditional mass media audiences have declined with the arrival of newer, more specialized forms of niche media (for example, television channels devoted entirely to shopping, news, or travel). Clients are therefore increasingly unwilling to rely on a single medium or a combination of the traditional media to deliver their sales messages. Today they are more likely to use a much wider mix of all the different kinds of promotional material to try to sell their goods and services. Thus, for example, a bank launching a new credit card might employ a mix of billboard advertising, television ads, letters or phone calls to potential customers, leaflets in its bank lobbies, and low interest rates for an introductory trial period.

Corporate advertising

Not all advertising is aimed at the individual consumer. Much of it occurs on an industrial, business-to-business, or government-to-business basis and appears only in the specialized or "trade" press—such as *Broadcast, Business Week,* or *Travel Trade Gazette*—or takes place at exhibitions, trade fairs, and similar gatherings. Here the customers at whom the advertising is aimed are not individuals buying for themselves or for their families. They are executives and officials making business

17% OF TRAVELLERS WILL FORGET SOMETHING ANYWAY.

No matter how you pack, there's often that small but essential item that gets left behind. Like a toothbrush, a comb or a razor. That's why at Holiday Inns we provide those items we know our guests most often forget.

We call it our "Forget Something?" programme. It's just a small example of our big commitment to service. So next time you travel, why not give us a call? And take a load off your mind.

STAY WITH SOMEONE WHO REALLY KNOWS YOU. ※ Holiday Inn

In today's highly mobile world, a great deal of advertising promotes travel-related services.

decisions about the purchase of items such as raw materials, machinery, and office equipment, or services such as software design, staff training, and market research.

How hard can it be to say no to a drink?

DRINKING AND DRIVING WRECKS LIVES.

Much government-sponsored, public information advertising is devoted to warning us of life's dangers. In recent years, such advertisements have become much more hard-hitting. In this case, the message being conveyed concerns the serious injuries that can be caused by drinking and driving.

Not all advertising is designed directly to promote and sell goods and services. Large companies—particularly those involved in potentially consumer-unfriendly activities such as nuclear energy and the oil business—spend a great deal of money promoting what is called a positive "corporate image" in order to encourage people to trust and respond positively towards the company itself. If such an advertising strategy is successful, it not only reassures existing customers and attracts new ones, but also appeals to actual or potential investors.

A great deal of advertising, however, is not commercially motivated at all. Government departments spend vast sums of money on information campaigns of one kind or another. These include campaigns designed to encourage people to conserve energy, prevent forest fires, eat healthy, and put up smoke detectors in their homes; or to discourage them from taking illegal drugs, driving under the influence of alcohol, and risking infection with the AIDS virus.

Nor is it only governments that engage in advertising campaigns of this type: charities such as Oxfam and the Red Cross advertise in order to both raise funds and heighten public awareness of particular issues. Similarly, campaign groups such as Greenpeace and the Anti-Nazi League use advertising to promote their causes, as do the mainstream political parties, especially at election times.

Finally, by placing advertisements in quality newspapers such as the *New York Times* and the *Toronto Star*, companies attempt to recruit new employees—and also, incidentally, provide a crucial source of revenue for such papers. Given the increased demand for highly skilled workers and business executives, recruitment agencies of one kind or another have become substantial press advertisers in recent years.

> "Half the money I spend on advertising is wasted, and the trouble is I don't know which half."
> *British soap magnate Lord Leverhulme (1851-1925)*

Voluntary groups and charities frequently make effective use of advertisements in their efforts to raise public consciousness about specific issues. This ad warns parents not to buy their children dogs as presents.

TOYS AREN'T US.

A DOG IS FOR LIFE, NOT JUST FOR CHRISTMAS.
National Canine Defence League

PLANNING AN ADVERTISING CAMPAIGN

A dvertising involves spending money, and, in the case of large organizations, a vast amount of it. But anybody thinking of selling a product or service first of all needs to ask themselves if advertising will actually help them to do so.

The four Ps

Selling involves achieving the right balance between the four different elements of what is known as the "marketing mix," or the "four Ps."
- Product—having a marketable product or service to sell in the first place
- Price—selling it at a competitive price

This billboard advertisement puts the brand name before the public with a single image used in an eye-catching way.

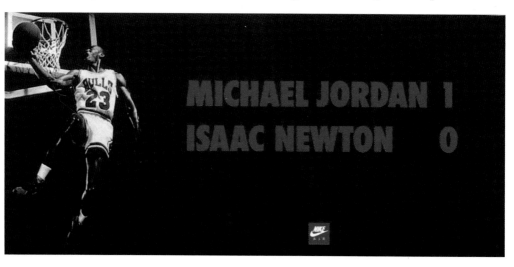

MICHAEL JORDAN 1
ISAAC NEWTON 0

NIKE
AIR

- Place—ensuring that customers can find it easily
- Promotion—presenting it in an attractive way

Advertising is a crucial part of the promotion process, the other elements of which are personal selling, sales promotion (such as special offers, loyalty cards, and competitions), and the wider business of public relations, which involves encouraging the media to distribute favorable information about a company and its products or services.

Advertising is attractive to those with something to sell because it can deliver messages rapidly and directly to large numbers of people. Advertising can be spread across a wide range of different media, creating all-pervasive campaigns in which the message in one medium is reinforced by those in others. For example, you may go to the supermarket and encounter a special promotion for a new breakfast cereal. In the car on the way home, you may see a billboard for that cereal and hear an advertisement for it on the radio. When you arrive, you might find that a free sample has been put into your mailbox, and when you sit down to watch television and commercials come on in the middle of your favorite program, there it is again.

The moving images of commercials help to convey advertising messages in a more elaborate way.

If it's created with flair and imagination, advertising can be a source of pleasure in itself. It not only creates a positive, sales-inducing mood around whatever is being advertised, but, at the same time, boosts the image of the producer or provider as well.

A crucial role

Advertisements for goods and services perform a whole range of different functions.

- Creating customer awareness of a new product or service
- Constructing or maintaining a "brand image"
- Announcing special offers of one kind or another
- Building long-term customer loyalty and confidence
- Combatting the negative claims of competitors
- Keeping existing customers in the face of competition
- Converting the customers of rival brands

Before it enlists the help of an advertising agency, a company wanting to run a campaign should have a clear idea of what it wants to promote, who it hopes to reach, and how much it has to spend.

Advertising is not something that businesses undertake lightly or in a hit-and-miss fashion. It is a major area of expenditure, and the success or failure of their products or services can hinge on the effectiveness of an advertising campaign. It demands careful analysis, decision-making, and planning. Clear objectives need to be set from the start, a budget decided upon, the right messages have to be created and then targeted at the appropriate sections of the population, and the advertising must be coordinated with all other forms of promotional activity. This means that any business needs employees to oversee the advertising of its products or services.

Shopping for an agency

Responsibility for advertising management within a business depends on the size and complexity of the organization and the emphasis it places on advertising within the overall marketing mix. A small organization in which advertising is relatively unimportant may not have an advertising staff at all, and advertising may be one of the sales director's tasks. On the other hand, a large company producing consumer goods or offering financial services will most certainly have an in-house advertising department. This department will generally have two main functions: to decide which advertising agency or agencies to use and to supervise their operations; and to buy in or provide services not offered by the agency or agencies.

The architecture of the Chiat/Day/Mojo agency in Venice, California, is in itself an advertisement for the company's visual flair.

The advertising department of a large company is the responsibility of the advertising manager (also known as the communications, brand, publicity, product, or marketing services manager). One of his or her key roles is to decide whether the services of an advertising agency are required, and, if so, which services. Once it has been decided to use an agency, a list of possible candidates is drawn up, usually with the involvement of the company's marketing director and managing director. This is known as "shopping" for an agency.

Some companies have long-standing relationships with particular agencies; however, in today's volatile media environment, few stay with one agency for more than about three years. Most agencies are employed on short-term contracts, and it is quite common for one agency to try to lure away another's clients.

The pitch

If a company is searching for an agency, it will look at the current crop of advertisements, identify the agencies that produce those it likes the best, and ask that agency to make a "pitch" for the job. A pitch is a presentation detailing what the agency would do with the client's product or service in terms of creative work, targeting the right customers, buying advertising space, and so on. On the basis of what it feels to be the most convincing pitch, the company will then select an agency.

The advertising manager needs to know how different agencies work, what services they provide, and how they are paid for their services. (This will be explored in more detail in the next chapter.) Most importantly, since the success of a company's advertising campaign depends on a harmonious relationship with its agency, the manager must know how to work successfully with agency staff members. This is not always easy. Those on the creative side of an agency's work tend to regard themselves as the experts and to take a personal interest in their proposals and ideas. These, however, may not always match the client's own expectations. Alternatively, the agency may feel it has been presented with a product that is not easily salable, or that the client wants to aim it at the wrong group of

The pitch: the agency tries to persuade the client to use its services to create their advertising campaign.

potential consumers. Such situations are particularly delicate ones for the advertising manager to deal with and have, in fact, led many a client and agency to part ways.

The brief

The best way to keep such a situation from arising in the first place is for the client to give the agency the clearest possible idea from the outset of what it requires from the agency: this is known as the "brief." This should not simply concern the product or service itself, but should also describe the company's intended market, its desired corporate image, and so on. In general, the earlier the agency can be involved in the development of the new product, the better it will be able to advise on an effective advertising campaign. However, it usually enters the overall marketing campaign around its halfway point, which is too late to be concerned with the more fundamental aspects of branding, package design, pricing, and deciding at which part of the market the product should be aimed.

The briefing process needs to be a continuous one, with the agency given every opportunity to become familiar with and understand exactly what it is being asked to advertise. At the same time, the client needs to monitor and approve every stage of the advertising campaign, from the design and production of the advertisements to the buying of advertising space and time in the various media. Above all, the client needs to be assured that the initial brief is being adhered to, and that the work is being carried out within the agreed budget. All of these matters are the responsibility of the advertising manager, who should ideally regard the agency as an extension of his or her own department. In particular, he or she must understand the roles of the various agency departments and personnel, and especially be able to work harmoniously with the agency account manager or executive, whose role is described in the following chapter.

Clearly, then, advertising management, which involves organizing, buying, and supervising, requires a wide range of quite different skills. Managers must be able to supervise advertising personnel without undermining their professional independence. They also must be able to locate and deal with the appropriate outside agencies and suppliers.

Finally, since advertisements are placed in a wide range of media, including newspapers, magazines, radio, television, and the cinema, the advertising manager should have a knowledge of artwork, printing, photography, film, and video in a world in which media technologies are changing at an ever-faster rate.

Advertisements for Benetton clothes are clearly aimed at the international youth market.

HOW AN ADVERTISING AGENCY WORKS

The advertising agency occupies the middle ground between those with goods or services to sell and the media in which they wish to advertise. Obviously a local, small business doesn't need an agency in order to advertise in the local press, and someone trying to sell their car through an advertisement in their local paper doesn't need the services of an advertising agency. In the United States, local car dealerships often run advertising campaigns on local television featuring their own sales staff—often with excruciating results. But a company planning an expensive, nationwide, or international sales campaign is more than likely to employ an agency's valuable skills in planning and executing the advertising campaign and buying the right kind of media space.

Different skills

Some agencies offer a "full service" to their clients, but today it is quite common for clients to use purely creative agencies, sometimes known as "hot shops" or "a la carte" agencies, to design and produce the advertising campaign. The clients will then use "media shops" or "media independents" to purchase the media space in which to display the advertisements. With so many different kinds of media now available in

Media Fact

The Unique Selling Proposition

In the early 1940s, U.S. ad executive Rosser Reeves developed the idea of the Unique Selling Proposition (U.S.P.). As he explained: "Each advertisement must say to each reader, 'Buy this product, and you will get this specific benefit: one that the competition either cannot, or does not, offer.'" Much "hard sell" advertising, which attempts to influence the consumer in a very direct, head-on fashion, is still based on this idea.

which to advertise, and the consequent rise in advertising costs, clients may feel it advisable to shop around for different skills at different agencies in order to purchase those they consider best for them at the most reasonable prices. On the other hand, using the full service agency has the advantages of "one-stop shopping" and enables client and agency to develop a close and mutually beneficial working relationship.

So why don't the providers of goods and services simply create and sell their own advertisements? The answer is that agencies offer their clients teams of highly skilled experts and save the clients the expense of having to employ such people full-time. These skills may be in design, production, market research, or buying advertising space in the media (known as "media buying"). From the media's point of view, the system's advantage is that media companies have to deal with a relatively small number of experienced agencies as opposed to a vast number of possibly inexperienced individual advertisers.

A busy office in a full service agency. Full service agencies, as their name suggests, offer a full range of services to their clients.

The commission system

The main source of income for larger agencies used to be commission. Agencies bought space and time for their clients in the various media, and, in return, these media paid the agencies commission, essentially a financial reward for bringing them customers. Today, the commission system still exists and is generally favored by the media as it makes life easier for them. But many agencies now charge their clients a fee to cover all the costs incurred during the creation and production of a campaign, and if any commission has been received from the media, this is deducted from the fee.

An advertising agency may consist of a few individuals, or it may be a vast, multi-national corporation employing thousands of people around the world. A full agency will offer the following services to the client (also known as the "account").

Graphic design skills are extremely important in the advertising world. Here, a designer marks up a rough visual for a print ad with colored markers.

Account management

This is the main area of communication between the client and the agency. Account executives or managers are responsible for agreeing on an appropriate brief with the client(s) for whom they are working and then ensuring that this is passed on to and fully understood by all the appropriate people and departments within the agency.

Creative

The task of the creative department is to turn the brief that has been agreed upon with the client into an attractive, persuasive advertising message or, in the case of a campaign appearing in a number of different media, series of messages. The key personnel on the creative team are primarily copywriters and designers.

Media

The media department consists of media planners and media buyers, although these roles are sometimes combined in smaller agencies. Media planners are experts in the planning of "media schedules." This means that they know which media to choose in order to reach particular target audiences most effectively, and how to use these to greatest advantage. Media buyers negotiate with the chosen media to buy the best advertising space or time at the most reasonable rates.

Traffic and production

Production refers to the various processes whereby ideas and designs for advertisements are turned into actual artwork that can be delivered to the printers, or into a film that is ready for screening, and so on. The crucial task of keeping track of each stage of the process of creating advertisements, from initial briefing to final production, is known as "traffic."

Account planning

Formerly this job would have either been carried out by account management or farmed out to specialist market research companies. Today, many agencies employ specialist staff members to research the "bigger picture," the wider context, within which specific advertising campaigns will fit. It is their responsibility to understand how societies, and especially patterns of consumption, are changing. They do this by keeping abreast of, and often commissioning, market research such as consumer surveys. Armed with the latest information about the world in which his or her client's products or services are about to be launched, the account planner is particularly useful in helping to decide the most effective overall strategy for the campaign. Once a campaign is in progress, the account planner also monitors its degree of success, and the valuable information gathered is used in the planning of future campaigns.

The Account Executive

The account executive, who may be responsible for one or more accounts, is the primary point of contact between the agency and the client. He or she interacts with the different agency departments handling the client's business and keeps, runs, and develops the client's business with the agency. As such, the account executive must understand the client's needs and interpret these to the agency, as well as present the agency's ideas, proposals, and work to the client. He or she is the business person in this all-important relationship, agreeing on and supervising the budgets, negotiating fees, making sure that deadlines are met, participating in discussions about campaign strategy and target markets, and discussing with media planners the appropriate choice of media in which to place the advertisements.

The role of account executive is a delicate, diplomatic balancing act, but his or her ultimate responsibility is to keep the account. The client expects the account executive not only to know about the client's business, but to be enthusiastic about it, too. He or she needs to be well aware of the activities of the client's competitors and to keep fully informed about the issues facing the client's particular area of business. At the same time, colleagues in the agency will expect the account executive to know not only about advertising, but also about the popular culture of which it is a part.

The creative department will expect the account executive to have seen the hottest new director's latest commercial, and the media planners will assume that he or she has read the latest articles on the current state of the media by the most reliable commentators and analysts. And all the while the account executive's bosses will want to know if he or she is going to meet their budget.

The account executive keeps clients informed about the development of their campaigns.

THE CREATIVE PROCESS

" . . . the time has come when advertising has in some hands reached the status of a science."
Claude Hopkins in Scientific Advertising, *1923*

During the early part of the 20th century, it was sometimes thought that advertising worked according to scientific principles, and that success in advertising lay in discovering and then applying these principles. Today, in spite of the vast amount spent on market research, and especially on trying to measure the degree of success of various advertising campaigns, most advertisers would probably agree that it is a much more random business than it was originally thought to be.

The account management department plays a key role in the relationship between the client and the agency.

A mix of skills

Advertising is in fact a process in which creativity and imagination play a key role, but which also involves a great deal of calculation,

research, and business sense. It is also extremely expensive, and therefore not something to be embarked upon in a casual, hit-and-miss fashion. It's not a matter of simply following a creative person's instincts or hunch, nor just a question of designing attractive pictures or coming up with bright ideas expressed in clever words. Rather it's a way of expressing certain ideas in such a way as to attract and interest particular groups of people and to encourage them to react in a particular fashion—namely, by buying a particular product or service. It is therefore especially important that the client and the account management present those creative people responsible for designing an advertising campaign with the clearest possible "creative brief" from the outset.

The creative team needs to be fully briefed by account management about the advertisement they will be responsible for producing. Here, members of both groups are exploring a film location.

Computers play a vital role in the production of artwork for advertisements. Here, a graphic designer is preparing a "rough" for a client presentation.

Prospect definition

A good creative brief allows the creative person to organize his or her thinking along the relevant lines instead of just trying to pluck an idea out of the air. In particular, it needs to explain why the client is advertising at all (launching a new product or trying to get an existing one to appeal to a different section of the market, for example) and what the advertising is expected to achieve (such as a change in consumer attitude or perception). Most important of all is "prospect definition." This means that the brief must make it absolutely clear which particular sections of the market the advertising should target, since no product or service can be all things to all people. And finally, the brief must indicate the "reason for being," the "why to buy," of the product or service being advertised.

Across the media

Today, most mainstream products are advertised via a whole range of different media—radio, television, newspapers, magazines, the Internet, and so on. All these media have different creative requirements, and what works in one medium will not necessarily work in another. For example, an advertisement that depends on moving images for its effect, such as an ad for a sports car, is hardly likely to work on the radio. So the way in which the advertising message is expressed may vary considerably from medium to medium, although all the messages in the various media have to be conceived as part of the same overall campaign by those responsible for the advertisements. Ideally, then, the creative process of designing the advertisements and the commercial business of buying advertising space in the media should proceed hand-in-hand.

As noted in the previous chapter, the work of designing an advertising campaign is undertaken by either the creative department of a "full service" advertising agency or by a creative agency. Both tend to work in similar ways. Like any business activity, and especially one tied to tight media deadlines, a creative department needs a degree of structure and control to ensure that things get done, and done on time. However, because designing and producing advertising is also a creative and imaginative process, it requires flexibility and freedom as well.

The art director and the photographer discuss the images taken during a photo shoot.

The creative team

The key members of the creative team are art directors and copywriters, who work together to come up with the concepts, words, and images that will form the heart of the advertising campaign. Formulating the main ideas for the campaign and perfecting the overall concept usually takes about three weeks. Once this is done the art director will concentrate more on the visual aspects of the campaign, creating the series of still images (known as "storyboards") that serve as a rough map of the cinema or television advertisements, and producing preliminary sketches of the print or poster advertisements. Meanwhile, the copywriter focuses more on producing the text, although still working closely with the art director. The text itself might be a short slogan for a poster or press advertisement, a longer body of text for a direct-mailing, or the script for a radio or television slot.

There have been numerous attempts to formulate "rules" for the production of effective

The creative team presents the roughs to the account group for their approval.

The Creative Director

The creative director oversees the various art director/copywriter creative teams, of which a large agency will have several. Each may be working on a number of accounts at once. Although these teams originate their own campaign ideas, they discuss these with the creative director as they go along, and he or she will generally act as a sounding board and helpful critic. Long before any creative ideas are revealed to the client, the creative director and the creative team will have agreed together that these ideas properly fulfill the brief, that everyone is fully satisfied with the work they've produced, and that it all meets the agency's high creative standards. This is important not simply in order to please the client and retain the client's business in the future, but also because the agency needs to maintain its reputation, and thus its ability to attract new business in an extremely competitive industry.

At this stage the creative work is unveiled to the client, who—the creative director and his or her team profoundly hope—will approve of it. If not, a certain amount of "selling" or persuasion may take place (this is usually done either by the creative or account manager), or the creative work has to be modified to meet the client's wishes. Once the work has been agreed upon, a budget will be negotiated (if it has not already been agreed at the brief stage), and the campaign will finally enter the production stage.

As well as supervising the creative teams, the creative director also works on his or her own campaigns—usually prestigious accounts of particular importance to the agency—with art directors and copywriters. He or she has greater contact with the clients than more junior creative staff members, working directly with them at regular presentations and meetings. He or she also discusses new accounts and projects with account managers and directors. Most creative directors sit on the agency's board, both in order to represent their own department and to influence the business strategy for the agency as a whole. Finally, the creative director is responsible for ensuring effective communication between account management and the creative and production staffs.

The creative director examines artwork produced by the campaign team.

Images play a key role in most advertisements, so it is crucial to choose the right ones. Here the art director examines transparencies on a lightbox.

Media Fact

Hidden persuaders

In 1957, Vance Packard wrote his famous book *The Hidden Persuaders*, in which he included advertising among the ways "many of us are being influenced and manipulated—far more than we realize—in the patterns of our everyday lives. Large-scale efforts are being made, often with impressive success, to channel our unthinking habits, our purchasing decisions, and our thought processes by the use of insights gleaned from psychiatry and the social sciences. Typically these efforts take place beneath our level of awareness, so that appeals which move us are often, in a sense, 'hidden.'"

copy, but many successful advertisements have cast doubt on these by resolutely disregarding them! However, in his 1963 book *Confessions of an Advertising Man*, David Ogilvy laid out three principles for advertising headlines that still hold true today.

(a) Attract attention
(b) Win the reader's interest and involvement
(c) Make the reader want to read on because he or she feels it will be worthwhile to do so

From this it can be seen that good advertising copy follows much the same principles as effective popular journalism, such as using headlines and opening sentences that are eye-catching, bold, colloquial, get straight to the point, and hold the reader's attention.

The Account Planner

Every advertisement is aimed at a particular audience. The more the advertiser knows about that audience, the better the chance both of reaching it and of persuading members of the audience to buy the client's product or service. It is the job of the account planner to find out as much as possible about the target audience, to discover what makes it tick.

Account planners must be psychologists, sociologists, and futurologists; they not only need to know what's fashionable now, but what is likely to be in the future. For this they need to study the latest newspaper, magazine, and academic journal articles, and to keep up-to-date with the most recent market research. If the research they need has not yet been carried out, then they need to commission it themselves. They have to know not only how to gather data but also how to draw useful conclusions from it.

More than anything else, the account planner is concerned with advertising's effectiveness, and his or her knowledge of this can be of invaluable help to the creative staff. By understanding everything there is to know about the audience for a particular advertisement, the account planner can help his or her creative colleagues to reach it and to appeal to it in the most effective way. There are, however, creative staff members who regard planners as nuisances employed to produce research that "kills" their bright (but impractical) ideas!

Account planners are natural strategists—people who can see the big picture and plan accordingly. They are a stage removed from the day-to-day business objectives of the account manager and from the pressure that he or she is frequently under from the clients (who often think they know best). This means that the account planner can contribute a much-needed element of informed objectivity to discussions between agency and client about how best to reach and appeal to the target audience. For all these reasons, then, account planning, though a relatively recent development, is now regarded as an invaluable asset to most English-speaking advertising markets.

The account planner needs to keep in touch with current trends—and look to the future.

BUYING TIME AND SPACE

Those with goods and services to sell need the mainstream media in which to advertise, and media that are wholly or partly funded by advertising need advertisers in order to survive. Buying and selling advertising space is therefore a crucially important matter for advertising agencies and media owners alike. Media space is a commodity that is traded like any other. The goal is to buy the right amount of space that reaches the right people at the right time, and to do so as cheaply as possible.

The media department of an agency is responsible for choosing the media in which advertisements for its clients' goods and services will appear, and for negotiating the best deals with those media. As the number and variety of media outlets have skyrocketed, and as competition between them for advertising revenue has grown more intense, so the business of "media buying" has become more complex. With more and more magazines to read, television channels to watch, and Web sites to surf, it has become harder and harder to find the best way of reaching any given audience.

A good deal of the work of the media department consists of research—particularly into media audience figures.

The media department needs to keep fully up-to-date with television audience figures.

For the last decade, media departments are where the action has been in the advertising industry. With clients eager to keep their advertising costs from rising still further, pressure has mounted on agencies to negotiate ever more fiercely the price of advertising space. Along with the breakdown of the commission system described earlier, these developments have led to the rise of the specialist media buying company. Some of these are off-shoots of full-service agencies, such as Zenith, which was formed out of Saatchi & Saatchi, but others are entirely independent organizations.

Media independents
A media independent, like the media department of a full-service agency, performs two major functions. The first is media planning, which involves selecting the media to be used for particular campaigns. The second is media buying, which means negotiating with the media for advertising space at the best rates for the client.

Advertisers need to know as much as they can about consumers' current habits, and often use focus groups in order to discover more about them.

At the outset of the campaign, a media plan is drawn up between the client and the media planner. The client will normally have clear views about which media they wish to use and know how much they want to spend in the different forms of media, and the media planner will offer further advice on these matters. The most important questions to be answered at this stage are: what are the campaign objectives, who are the target customers, what are competitors doing, and what will be the most cost-effective buy to deliver the best and greatest amount of coverage at the lowest price.

Clearly certain media are better suited to certain kinds of advertising than to others. For example, cigarette advertising is not allowed on television, so tobacco companies have to advertise on the sides of racing cars, in magazines, and on billboards. Magazines have long lead times (that is, they need artwork and copy well in advance of publication) so they are not suited to campaigns launched at short notice. Advertising aimed at creating a positive and attractive image for a product or service generally needs the full resources of the moving image; think, for example, of advertisements for Coca-Cola or Nike shoes. Free samples or discount coupons that can be cut out of newspapers and magazines may be the best way to encourage people to try new products. And so the list goes on. Generally, however, planners favor spreading advertising among a number of different media, with the advertisements carefully tailored to make the most of the possibilities offered by each. Not only does this enable more people to be reached, but it also helps to boost the significance of the product or service in the public eye.

Coverage and frequency

However, advertisers do not have limitless resources, and so financial factors also play a major role in deciding the choice of media and the number of occasions on which the advertisements will appear. It is the amount of money that the advertiser is prepared to spend that ultimately sets limits on the all-important matters of the coverage and the frequency of the campaign. Coverage is the number of people in the target market actually reached. For print media, this is measured in circulation, or the number of issues sold; for television, it is measured in ratings, or estimated numbers of viewers. Frequency refers to the number of times that the target audience has an opportunity to see an advertisement in a campaign. Clearly, what advertisers want to achieve is both the

Auto racing is an area in which cigarette advertising is still permitted.

greatest coverage of their target audience and the most frequent opportunities for them to see the advertising in question, and to do this at the lowest possible cost.

It should not be thought, however, that good coverage is simply a matter of reaching the largest possible number of people. What really counts, and never more so than in these days of marketing aimed at very specific sections of the total population, is reaching as many people as possible in the section at which you're aiming.

In the case of luxury goods and services, for example, this may be relatively small, but this is compensated for by the considerable buying power of the consumers of these goods. Equally, while some manufacturers such as Procter and Gamble may have repeated the same advertisements over a long period of time in order to emphasize the staying-power of certain brands, others have gained a great deal of exposure from one single advertisement. An example of the latter is the advertisement made by Apple Computers specifically for a Superbowl game that both reached a massive audience and became a news item in its own right.

Holidays give companies opportunities to advertise their goods and services in seasonal fashion.

Rocher is perfect for Valentines:
You'll fulfill the expectation of getting something round, shiny and gold.

FERRERO ROCHER

Luscious chocolate, crunchy hazelnut, crispy wafer and always in good taste.

The Media Planner

The media planner is responsible for finding both the particular section of the population with which the advertiser is most eager to communicate and the best means of doing so. This is a job that requires highly developed research skills and an intimate knowledge of the current media scene, as well as an understanding of current social trends, especially in the area of consumption and leisure time. The media planner needs to study the circulation figures of newspapers and magazines, estimated-viewer statistics for poster sites, viewing figures for television programs, and listening figures for radio stations. He or she also needs to gather as much data as possible on the target audience for the advertisement—for example, by consulting the databases of market research organizations.

There are certain questions the media planner needs to consider.
- Which media are most suited to the advertisement in question?
- Which should be the main, and which the supporting, media?
- How can these best be used?

Once the media planner has analyzed the available media and assessed their relative suitability for the advertisement in question, he or she puts together a proposal. This details which media the planner has selected, and when and how many times the advertisement should appear.

The planner then presents this proposal to the account manager and the client. The client will obviously have an opinion about the media choice, as will the account manager and the creative team. But ultimately the media planner will have the facts and figures to back up his or her case and to suggest that his or her plans will lead to the client's budget being spent in the most effective way possible.

The media planner needs to cultivate a wide range of useful contacts in the media world.

Frequency may be dictated by seasonal factors, too, such as Christmas or Mothers' Day. For example, there would be little point in featuring the Easter Bunny in advertisements planned to appear in July! You may also have noticed that the majority of press advertisements for consumer products appear on Fridays, the day when many people are paid and the day before the weekend, when the bulk of consumer spending takes place.

Bursts and drips

When thinking about the frequency with which advertisements in a campaign should appear, media planners and buyers often talk of "bursts" and "drips." "Burst" campaigns are concentrated into two or three weeks. Aiming at high coverage and frequency, they usually spread across a number of media and are used mainly to help launch new products and services. Meanwhile, "drip" campaigns are staggered over a number of months, with fairly low frequency advertising. They are generally intended to remind consumers of a brand's positive qualities. In fact, most advertisers combine the two strategies, bursting occasionally and steadily dripping in between.

When media planners or buyers need to work out the rough cost of media buying, they use the "rate cards" that all magazines, newspapers, and commercial broadcasters make available to advertisers. These list the cost of buying advertising time or space, and the prices on rate cards reflect the size of the audience for a particular part of the broadcasting schedule or of the readership of a particular publication. On the whole, the bigger the audience or readership, the higher the prices, but, as mentioned earlier, advertisers may also be prepared to pay high prices for reaching smaller but richer-than-average audiences. However, when it comes to the actual deal, the media buyer ought to be able to negotiate a reasonable discount on the quoted rates. The media offer discounts to attract new advertisers, to keep valued existing ones, or to undercut competitors.

Rates and revenue

Of course, the planners and buyers do not make these decisions alone. Every newspaper, magazine, and commercial broadcaster has a busy advertisement sales department whose job

Glamorous models, male and female, are frequently featured in filmed advertising images.

it is to attract as much advertising revenue as possible, and media owners compete ruthlessly with one another in the matter of advertising rates. Media sales representatives from these companies are constantly on the lookout for new business and are eager to find out when new advertising campaigns are going to begin and which agencies will be looking to buy space and where. It is their job to know the people responsible for buying media space, and to encourage them to send business their way.

Advertising is bought in different units. In newspapers, it is bought by the single column inch; in magazines, by fractions of a page (quarter-page, half-page, etc.); and in broadcasting, by time. In newspapers, space in certain parts, such as the front pages and special sections and supplements, is much more

Images of parents and children are often used to create positive associations in advertisements for goods and services.

expensive than in others. In television, the rate card divides the day into breakfast (6:00 A.M. to 9:30 A.M.), pre-peak (9:30 A.M. to 6:00 P.M.), peak (6:00 P.M. to 10:30 P.M.) and late (10:30 P.M. to 6 A.M.). Different rates apply to different segments of the day, with peak times obviously commanding the highest rates. Even here, however, there are variations, with "spots" at the beginning and end of commercial breaks costing more than those in the middle.

A market researcher gathers information from a member of the public.

It can also cost more to advertise during some special programs. Commercials during a Superbowl, World Series game, Academy Awards show, or important political debate are some examples of very expensive advertising time.

The Media Buyer

The media buyer negotiates with the sales representatives of media organizations to buy space for advertisements on behalf of his or her clients. The media buyer's skill lies in getting the best space at the lowest possible rates. He or she manages huge budgets, often amounting to millions of dollars a year. The media buyer generally specializes in either press or broadcast buying but also needs to be able to formulate effective buying strategies for major campaigns that take place across a wide range of different media. If the buyer works for a media independent, he or she deals directly with the clients; at a full-service agency, he or she works with the account planners and managers.

Like the media planner, the media buyer needs to keep fully abreast of current media research, especially audience figures for the different media, and to be fully informed about the latest work on consumer attitudes and behavior. He or she works closely with media sales representatives, who, in particular, keep the buyer informed about forthcoming features in their media that might tie in well with a specific advertising campaign. When media buyers are negotiating for space, the kinds of questions that they consider are:

- What days of the week are most suitable for running the advertisement?
- In which section of a newspaper or magazine should it appear?
- What time(s) of day should it appear on radio and/or television?
- Is the price right?

The media buyer's job does not end with the buying of advertising space. Once the advertisement is up and running, the buyer checks that it has appeared in the right places and at the right times as agreed beforehand with the various media. He or she uses the resources of market research agencies to check the amount of coverage that each appearance of the advertisement actually achieved. This information is also used in the planning of future campaigns.

The media buyer needs to be extremely well informed about the current media scene, and to be familiar with the latest research into media trends.

PRODUCTION

In the 1950s and 1960s, most of the work of actually producing finished advertisements was carried out in-house by advertising agencies, the largest of which had their own photographers, filmmakers, illustrators, art directors, and so on. However, maintaining specialist, well-paid staff members on a permanent, full-time basis became more and more expensive, and the media explosion of the 1980s and 1990s called for an ever-wider range of different media production skills. Because of these developments, the actual making of advertisements has increasingly been farmed out to production specialists. On occasion, certain clients who would normally use an agency are now by-passing the middle-man altogether and dealing directly with production companies of one kind or another.

New technology

Until the early part of the 20th century, all advertising was in printed form. Now, although it needs to be borne in mind that most promotional messages of one kind or another are still transmitted in print, there is a whole host of other media at the advertiser's disposal. The number of commercial radio and television stations has increased dramatically. And the development of commercial telephone services, fax machines, e-mail, and Web sites (in other words, what is now commonly known as "e-commerce") has also opened up possibilities for advertisers to communicate with people in a more direct, personalized, and above all interactive fashion. This makes the process less

The contemporary advertiser will take full advantage of the possibilities offered by the Internet. Here, graphic artists work on designing an advertising Web site.

of a one-way affair and gives the consumer more of a chance to respond in a personal fashion. Advertisers today have many more media in which to advertise, but, at the same time, advertising costs in traditionally key areas such as newspapers, magazines, and television have risen steadily as media production costs have climbed with the introduction of new and more elaborate technology.

At the same time, many producers, retailers, and service providers have begun to lose faith in the effectiveness of conventional forms of above-the-line advertising and have turned increasingly to below-the-line forms. The result of all this is that the amount that companies spend on traditional media advertising is currently dropping sharply. In such a difficult situation, it becomes more important than ever that the right advertisement is produced for the right medium, and that advertisements are produced as economically as possible.

In the previous chapter we saw how crucial design and copywriting to the success of an advertising campaign. However, the best artwork and text can be ruined by poor production. This is the process of turning a set of ideas into something that can be read in a paper or brochure, seen on billboards, heard on the radio, or viewed on a television or computer screen.

Traditionally, the production stage in the case of the printed media consisted largely of ensuring that the writer's and art director's intentions lost as little as possible in the process of translation into print. However, with rapid advances in computer technology enabling what is known as "desktop publishing," the line between design and production has become increasingly blurred. It is no longer possible to draw a hard and fast distinction between the creative (design) and mechanical (production) aspects of advertisement production. This process has been further accelerated by the arrival of digital technology, which enables images and text to be

The client and agency staff watch a demonstration of a Web site advertisement.

The Production Assistant

The production department of a large agency may work on around 150 advertisements a week, and production assistants (PAs) are assigned many different tasks on a variety of accounts. It is the PA's job to work with the more senior production staff members and to help them in the all-important task of turning creative concepts into finished advertisements. The role of the PA is mainly administrative, although a particularly skilled PA may be entrusted with a limited amount of creative work. It is therefore perhaps not surprising to discover that PAs are frequently recruited from the upper secretarial ranks of the advertising agency, which means that this is a job in which women traditionally tend to predominate. It is, however, a good way into the creative side of the industry, and a role in which a great deal of useful skills and knowledge can be acquired.

The job varies according to whether it is in television production or print production, but in either case it is likely to involve dealing with numerous external suppliers, such as designers, typographers, printers, photo-reproducers, and paper manufacturers. Production assistants are expected to obtain estimates from these suppliers and to ensure that they are fully briefed about any work they are doing for the agency. The PA also checks regularly on and records the progress of that work, and makes sure that all supplies and finished work are delivered on time.

It is also the PA's job to keep in touch with the media in which the advertisements are to be placed, checking matters such as the size of the space available on a poster site or in the press, the submission deadline, and the required format. He or she also needs to ensure that account managers have the rough drafts or sketches (also known as "mock-ups") of advertisements ready for the all-important client presentations. Finally, the PA checks all print advertisements for any mistakes or inaccuracies and ensures that their dimensions are exactly right before passing the work back to the senior production staff and creative teams for "signing off."

The production assistant needs to be a quick and intuitive learner so that he or she can build up a thorough knowledge of production terms and techniques. He or she must be literate, numerate, should possess excellent verbal and negotiating skills, and must be able to work well in a team. The PA also needs to appreciate the crucial importance to the industry of producing finely crafted, error-free advertisements with tight deadlines.

A production assistant's job is a good introduction to the world of advertising.

produced, manipulated, and modified on a computer with considerable ease, speed, and flexibility, as anybody who possesses a scanner on their home computer system will know.

The production of an eye-catching billboard ad is often a more elaborate process than just designing and printing a paper poster. It may even involve engineering and construction skills.

In the case of radio, film, video, and television, however, the creative process continues far beyond conceiving an idea and then putting it down on paper in script or storyboard form. To begin with, a production company needs to be chosen (unless the agency has in-house production facilities), and then the director, the most important member of the production team, has to be appointed. He or she will play a key role in choosing the other production staff members, as well as the actors.

Since the script and storyboard are simply the bare bones of the advertisement, the agency, through the original creative team, will be involved in detailed discussions with the production team about how they want the finished advertisement to look. Although the

The Production Manager

The role of the production manager is mainly budgetary and administrative rather than creative. The production manager is a "progress chaser" whose job it is to ensure that all the relevant tasks are carried out on time, within the budget, and to a high standard. Production managers are responsible for the overall process of producing each advertisement. In particular, they must schedule work efficiently, as both client and media deadlines are notoriously inflexible. They coordinate teams of production staff who will be working on a large number of different advertisements, all at different stages of completion and on different timetables.

As in the case of the production assistant, much of what the production manager actually does depends on whether the job is in television or print production. Whatever the case, the manager must first agree on a realistic budget for each project with each team, as well as with any external suppliers who may be involved, and, as the job progresses, must constantly check that this is being adhered to. Budgeting is an extremely complex and contentious matter; it can involve extremely large sums of money and calls for considerable skills not simply in numeracy but also in negotiating.

As the work on an advertisement continues, the production manager holds regular meetings with the team to check on their progress. Production is monitored at every stage. The production manager also communicates with the account manager, who relays any views that the client may have on the progress

of the advertisement's production. When the production work on an advertisement is finally completed, the production manager checks it thoroughly before passing it on to the production director to be "signed off." In the case of television production, this will involve examining visual and sound quality in particular; in the case of print production, points to be checked will include photographic reproduction, type size and font, color tone, and so on. The production manager will then need to ensure that all advertisements are sent to the appropriate media on time and in the correct format, and, finally, that they appear in the media as they were intended to look.

Apart from the day-to-day business of advertisement production, the production manager is also responsible for recruiting and training production assistants, as well as checking on their progress in the job.

The production manager checks and passes the final version of the advertisement before sending it off for publication.

agency will have had a budget in mind before approaching the production company, this figure may well have to be revised as a result of these initial discussions. An extremely detailed budget is then drawn up by the production company and negotiated with the agency.

Given the large number of different kinds of media in which advertisements appear, and the wide range of highly varied skills required to create them, it is difficult to describe a "typical" production job. Film and television commercials will have to be shot with a professional film crew, headed by the director. Radio commercials will need to be recorded in a studio with a range of technical staff, including sound engineers, and so on.

The production process, however, is only half the story. Once pre-production and shooting of, for example, a TV commercial are completed, post-production begins. Music and sound-effects need to be added to the actors' voices on the soundtrack, and graphics or special visual effects may be required. Then the film will have to be edited, not simply in order to reduce all the filmed material to the right length for the advertisement slot, but to get across the message in the most visually effective way. During all the numerous stages a filmed advertisement goes through during production, the original creative team is likely to be closely involved throughout the process to ensure that the creative brief is being adhered to at all times.

Following the shoot, editing is an important part of the production process.

GETTING A JOB IN THE INDUSTRY

Advertising is an extremely high-profile industry; agencies such as Saatchi & Saatchi are household names, and famous film directors such as Ridley Scott (*Alien*, *Gladiator*) and Alan Parker (*The Commitments*, *Evita*) began their creative lives in advertising. It can be a glamorous world, with plenty of foreign travel and other perks, and the best campaigns win prizes and wide recognition.

Given its public image, however inaccurate, it's hardly surprising that far more people apply to work in advertising than the industry actually needs. Advertising professionals are bombarded every day with résumés and portfolios from hopeful applicants. It is therefore vital that anyone who is thinking of trying to go into advertising finds out a good deal about the industry, and in particular what qualities and abilities applicants should possess.

Becoming informed

The first, obviously, is an interest in and passion for advertising. However, this should also be an informed interest and passion. There are various ways in which advertising hopefuls can inform themselves about the industry.
- Reading the trade press
- Reading books by industry professionals
- Searching the Internet for advertising-related Web sites

- Talking to any contacts that your friends or family may have in the industry
- Contacting the industry trade associations
- Reading, watching, listening to, and, above all, forming opinions about advertisements

Asking the right questions

You also need to begin to understand the distinctive characteristics of the different kinds of agencies within the industry. These are the kinds of questions you should be able to answer.
- Which are the top agencies?
- Who are their major clients?
- Which major campaigns have they been responsible for?
- What distinguishes different types of agencies from each other?
- Who are the leading figures in the industry?
- Which particular advertisements do you most like and dislike, and why?
- What are the current issues being discussed within the industry?

Many famous film directors started off in advertising— here we see Ridley Scott of Alien *and* Gladiator *fame.*

You should decide exactly which area of advertising interests you the most. You also need to be aware, though, that the advertising industry is changing as rapidly as the media in which it advertises. Working in advertising has always involved fast learning curves, but never more so than now. Traditional job boundaries on the creative side are breaking down, but it's also increasingly difficult to separate jobs neatly into self-contained "business" and "creative" categories. Many roles now demand both business acumen and creative flair.

Relevant qualifications

The kind of qualifications you need obviously depend on the kind of job in which you're interested, although obtaining a degree is advisable regardless. No particular subjects are required, although those such as management, economics, sociology, media studies, and psychology might suggest themselves as relevant to work in various different parts of the industry. If, however, you're set on a job specifically on the creative side, then a flair for writing or design is a must. Here a degree in creative writing or graphic design might be a good idea, but the most important thing of all will be a portfolio of excellent work.

There are specialist courses available to those interested in the creative aspects of advertising, although most of these will require prior academic qualifications. It's also worth pointing out that creative personnel are frequently hired in teams of two (often, but by no means always, a copywriter and an art director) so you'll need to find a

An account manager explains the importance of client presentation to a trainee production assistant, while another member of the production team looks on.

kindred spirit! In this respect, going to college or attending a specialist course can provide a very useful source of industry contacts. Incidentally, the best creative jobs are rarely advertised, so you will need to find a creative director who likes your work enough to take you on. This may be an internship during college, or it may be on a freelance basis (in other words, not as part of a company's permanent staff) after college.

If your initial application is among the few lucky ones to be selected, you will then be asked to attend an interview. Whatever kind of job interests you in advertising, you should have ready answers to the following questions.

- Why do you want to go into advertising?
- Why do you want to work for this company specifically?
- Which of the current crop of advertisements do you particularly like and dislike, and why?
- Where do you see yourself in 5 or 10 years' time?
- What media do you read, listen to, and watch?
- What challenges are you looking for?
- How has advertising changed in recent years, and how do you think it will continue to change in the future?

Finally, as in all efforts to find work, and especially work in such a sought-after area as advertising, be prepared for rejection. Being turned down doesn't mean that you are unsuited for an advertising career, it simply means someone thought that you weren't suited for a particular job in a particular company. As John Blakemore, advertising director of SmithKline Beecham, advises: "Never give up. A lot of the time it's about being in the right place at the right time. If you really want to get into the industry, keep knocking on doors."

> " . . . the most important thing for graduates is to talk to people in advertising and get them to explain how it works. . . . When you go to an agency, you must know the work. To turn up at an agency not knowing their work is just mad."
> *Will Harris, Board Director of advertising agency Abbott Mead Vickers*

GLOSSARY

brand image a particular image or impression of the brand

branding creating brand identity

colloquial using everyday language

concepts ideas

copywriters people whose job it is to write the text of advertisements

corporate image the kind of public image that a company wishes to project

desktop publishing small scale publishing that makes full use of computer technology

diversity difference

e-commerce business conducted via computer over the Internet

globalization the process whereby people, countries, companies, and organizations across the world become increasingly interconnected

intermediaries go-betweens

market research consumer surveys

market share percentage of the total market for a product or service that a company can claim as customers

peak times the most popular television viewing times

portfolios examples of people's work

sponsors those companies that have contributed to a television or radio program's budget

target audience the specific audience at which an advertisement is aimed

USEFUL ADDRESSES

Advertising Age Magazine
http://www.AdAge.com
711 Third Avenue
New York, NY 10017-4036

The Advertising Council
http://www.adcouncil.org
261 Madison Avenue, 11th Floor
New York, NY 10016

Advertising Educational Foundation
http://www.aef.com
220 East 42nd Street, Suite 3300
New York, NY 10017-5806

Adweek Magazine
http://www.adweek.com
770 Broadway
New York, NY 1003

The American Advertising Federation
http://www.aaf.org
Suite 500
1101 Vermont Avenue NW,
Washington, DC 20005-6306

American Advertising Museum
http://www.admuseum.org
211 NW Fifth Avenue
Portland, OR 97209

American Association of Advertising Agencies
http://www.aaaa.org
405 Lexington Avenue, 18th Floor
New York, NY 10174-1801

American Marketing Association
http://www.marketingpower.com
311 S. Wacker Drive, Suite 5800
Chicago, IL 60606

The Association of National Advertisers
http://www.ana.net
708 Third Avenue
New York, NY 10017-4270

Business Marketing Association
http://www.marketing.org
400 N. Michigan Avenue, 15th floor
Chicago, IL 60611

INDEX

Numbers in **bold** refer to illustrations.

above-the-line advertising 10-11, 50
account executive 24, 27, 29, **29**
account management 27, **30**, 31, **31**
account planner 28, 37, **37**
account planning 28
advertising agencies 6, 7, 8, 9, 10, 11, 21, **21**, 22, 23, 24, 25, 26, 27, 28, 29, 38, 39, 49, 53
advertising audiences 10, 15, 37, 42
advertising campaigns 20, 22, 23, 25, 27, 28, 30, 32, 33, 34, 40, 44
advertising engines 5
advertising manager 21, 22, 23, 24
art director 33, **33**, 34, 35, **36**

below-the-line advertising 10-11, 50
billboard 51, **53**
branding 11-12, **12**, **14**, 20, 23
brief, the 31, 32
briefing 23

classified ads 6
clients 6, 7, 8, 10, 15, 21, 22, 23, 26, 27, 29, 31, 32, 38, 39, 40
commission 7, 10, 11, 26-27

copywriter 27, 33, 34, 35
corporate advertising 15
corporate image-making 16, 23
creative department 27, **31**, 32, **34**, 35
creative director 35, **35**

designers 27, **27**, **32**,
display ads 6

focus groups **40**
full service agencies 8, 25, **26**, 39

hot shops 25

information advertising 16-17, **16-17**
Internet ads 6, **8**, 32, 51

magazines 6, 7, 8, 24, 32, 40
market research 28, 30, 41, **47**
market share 12
media
buyer 27, 28, 48, **48**
department 27, 38, **38**, 39, **39**
independents 25, 39
planner 27, 28, 40, 43, **43**
schedules 28
space 25, 28, 32, 38-48

newspapers 5, 6, 7, 8, 24, 32, 40, 46

niche marketing 13-14, **13**, 15, **24**

Ogilvy, David 36

Packard, Vance 36
Parker, Alan 56
pitching 22, **22**
post-production 55, **55**
production assistant 52
production department 28
production manager 54
prospect definition 32
public relations 19

radio 5, 6, 8, 10, 24, 32
rates 44-46
recruitment advertising 17

sandwich men 5, **5**
Scott, Ridley 56, **57**
soap operas 8
sponsorship 8, 47
storyboards 34, 53

taxes 7
television 5, 6, 8, 10, 24, 32, 47
through-the-line advertising 14
traffic 28

Unique Selling Proposition, 25